Lingerie in VOGUE

Lingerie *in* VOGUE

SINCE 1910

by Christina Probert

ABBEVILLE PRESS · PUBLISHERS · NEW YORK

ACKNOWLEDGMENTS

So many people have shared their talents with *Vogue* over the years: artists, photographers, designers, craftsmen, writers, but also *Vogue's* own editors whose perspicacious choices have shaped the magazine. I am grateful to Janet Reger, and to Betty Williams of Berlei who generously shared their knowledge of lingerie past and present. I am indebted to Alex Kroll, Editor of Condé Nast Books, for his guidance throughout, Georgina Boosey for her editorial wisdom, Liz Bauwens for the book's design, Anna Houghton for her patience in coping with pictorial and editorial hurdles.

C.P.

First published in Great Britain by Thames and Hudson
in association with British *Vogue*

© 1981 by The Condé Nast Publications Ltd.
First published in the USA in 1981 by Abbeville Press, Inc.

Library of Congress Cataloging in Publication Data
Main entry under title:

Lingerie in Vogue since 1910.

(Accessories in Vogue)
1. Lingerie—History—20th century.   2. Underwear—History—20th century.
3. Vogue—History—20th century.   .I. Probert, Christina.   II. Vogue.
GT2073.L56   391'.42'0904   81-14926
ISBN 0-89659-268-5 (pbk.)   AACR2

Cover. BV 1978 Alex Chatelain. *Janet Reger*. Back cover. FV 1915 Margaret Bull. *Lord & Taylor*. Page 2. AV 1917.

CONTENTS

Key to captions

Information is given in the following order: edition; year; artist or photographer; designer or maker (the last always in *italic*). Editions are identified by initials:

AV   American *Vogue*
BV   British *Vogue*
FV   French *Vogue*
IV   Italian *Vogue*
GV   German *Vogue*

INTRODUCTION

'Without foundations there can be no fashion.'
Christian Dior (1905–57)

Lingerie is the secret touch of exotica in every woman's wardrobe. The silks and satins, frills and furbelows, frothing laces are chosen not only for fashion's sake, not only to conform to the rules of etiquette, current morality and medical opinion, not only for the seduction of the male sex: women have always chosen lingerie which would express their most personal whims and fantasies, confident that only their maids and intimates would ever catch a glimpse of what *Vogue* described in 1916 as 'those bashful trifles that are born to blush unseen'.

But lingerie has always played a practical, as well as an aesthetic role, and during the late nineteenth and early twentieth centuries this caused bitter argument. The traditional view, that tight stays were beneficial to a woman's moral character and physical state, was challenged by groups such as the Pre-Raphaelites, with their uncorseted aesthetic dress, the Rational Dress Movement and the Healthy and Artistic Dress Union. The hygienic chemise or combination layer between the skin and the unwashable corset was one subject of dispute: Dr Jaeger in the 1880s was convinced that wool was best next to the skin, its porous nature permitting 'noxious exhalations' to disperse. Rivals appeared in the form of Aertex (pure cotton) in 1888 and Viyella (cotton and wool) in 1891. Within twenty years the need for this highly absorbent layer lessened, as corsets became more readily washable.

After the death of Queen Victoria fashion changed rapidly. The breadth of skirts was suddenly reduced, the body tightly sheathed, to the ankle, in layers. Lingerie altered to shape the fashionable 'S'-bend, which emphasized bottom and bosom in an overtly erotic way. The number of undergarments was reduced to achieve the slim line, and the fabrics used were lighter. By 1910 the bust was not supported or covered by corseting. 'Bust extenders' and 'bust shapers', antecedents of the modern 'bra', were at this stage little more than camisoles worn for decency. Whatever women had gained by the freeing of the bust, however, was immediately lost as the upper thigh was imprisoned, even boned, in the long corset necessary to achieve Poiret's long Empire line. 'The new cut', said *Vogue*, 'does away with all the humping effect over the abdomen and has a tendency . . . to reduce the flesh . . . leaving the bust in its natural position – really one of the prettiest lines of the feminine figure. . . . Some of the French modistes are even suggesting . . . gowns fitted without any bust supporter of any kind.'

Lace-edged, silky petticoat to wear by itself, or under the fashionable softly clinging clothes. B V 1979 Lothar Schmid, *La Perla/Courtenay*

1910

Bust supporter of double-faced satin ribbon, fitted with flexible whalebone. A V 1909. *Mme Gardner*

Camiknickers: 'a trifle of red voile-de-soie, black tulle, and black velvet.' B V 1916

Until the twenties corsetry was distinct from lingerie: the corset boned, unrelenting; the lingerie soft, pretty, frilly. The distinction began to blur as the two were often amalgamated: corsets became softer, and the term 'lingerie' incorporated both. The Suffragette movement focused attention on changes which were already taking place, and perhaps encouraged lingerie manufacturers to adapt their products swiftly. Medical research brought changes in corset structure. The Edwardian corset, which produced the infamous 'S'-bend, was discovered to distort the spine. By 1910 the shape of the corset was changing to produce a straighter, although equally rigid constriction. The mobility needed for carrying out strenuous war work stimulated further developments which continued after the war.

Fashion has always influenced changes in lingerie, each new look focusing on a particular silhouette. To achieve the ideal straight shape in the early twenties, for example, corsets were tightly laced, bust-flattening corsets likewise. It was only at the end of the twenties, when a more natural shape (absent since the early nineteenth century) returned to fashion, that manufacturers became aware of the variety in female figures: Berlei carried out a survey in Australia and subsequently produced lingerie tailored to five physical types. This was a great move towards improving the fit of the garment.

During the first twenty years of the century lingerie accounted for a quarter of one's dress allowance. By the thirties machine-made lingerie, in the same fine fabrics as the hand-made variety, had become popular. From this time, particularly after the Depression, women were no longer prepared to spend vast sums on lingerie, which was now mass-produced. As fitness became fashionable during the thirties, there was pressure on companies to produce smaller, lighter, better-fitting lingerie. Du Pont led the research, producing revolutionary new fibres: nylon, Lycra (Elastane). As fabrics clung increasingly to the body, emphasis moved from the fit of the garment to the fitness of the body. Ironically, in the fitness-conscious seventies, Edwardian bloomers and camisoles returned to fashion, but worn with no more foundation than a slim, well-exercised body.

Between 1910 and 1920 layers were extensively reduced in number, fullness and fabric weight. By 1911 slits or straps were added between waist and hem of the corset, enabling the wearer to sit easily. Later came the sports corset cut away over the upper thighs for still more movement, and a cotton mesh corset with just one bone at centre front. By 1913 all corsets were straight-fronted. Dancing corsets were made entirely from the new silk tricot, which struck 'a nice balance between too much of restraint and too much of freedom.' However, some constriction was still considered to be good for women; *Vogue* disapproved of the 'daring persons' who adopted the newest, brief sports corset for everyday wear.

Under the corset, the chemise gradually rose to knee level. In many cases it was replaced by the new shorter slim-cut combination. Similar in shape to the chemise, the corset cover had a low, rounded neckline held by threaded ribbons. It was gradually replaced, as the corset shrank, by a new garment, variously named the 'soutien-gorge', 'bust supporter' and 'brassière'. At first it was a simple shape in batiste, with front lacing or buttons. Later versions were lacy, ruffled, made from cambric with net insertions, cotton tricotrine, silk and satin, reaching the waist. Some even had shaped moulds to increase the bust (but gave no support to the breasts), which *Vogue* considered 'apt to give an artificial appearance'.

The decency formerly afforded by the long chemise was maintained by full drawers worn beneath the corset. There were many types: some were combined with the camisole or short chemise for wear underneath the corset, and later in a wider, shorter all-in-one as camiknickers. In 1914 there was a reaction against the new short 'culotte-knickers', and a brief return to fuller styles in finest silk chiffon to reduce bulk. Camiknickers became the norm, with straight bodices, narrow shoulder straps, lace flounces on their wide leg opening. The petticoat, vital to Victorian dress, lost favour during the early 1900s, but the long princess slip remained fashionable.

Negligees, boudoir gowns, tea gowns were the flowering of the *lingères'* art and innovation: pure, unbridled luxury, designed with a total disregard for practicality. 'Almost any young girl will confess', noted *Vogue* in 1916, 'that her greatest weakness is for the pretty things of the boudoir. Nothing caresses her to the same purring delight as a soft, silken peignoir or a fluffy matinée.' Tea gowns, which still had trains, were worn over corsets for entertaining the most intimate friends. Negligees and tea gowns in 1910 were lacy, in pastel silks, heavily embroidered with gold and silks adorned further with Madeira and baby Irish lace, jewelled buttons. Kimonos were popular throughout the decade. By 1917 nightwear was much lighter ('nightie' came into general usage), in pale silk, chiffon, and worn with the smart boudoir caps to insure against what *Vogue* described as the 'meanest badness a woman can do in all this big, bad world . . . to look ugly in bed'.

Decoration, colour and fabrics for lingerie varied from season to season. In 1910 tea gowns and negligees were in pastels, but underthings were usually white. Finer fabrics, easily laundered cottons in wartime, fine chiffons and crepe de chines were favourites. Corsets began the decade in batiste, brocaded satin, ending in lighter silk tricot; elastic panels were a new note. *Vogue* recommended the boudoir cap as the solution to every woman's problems: 'Madame has no need to fear . . . the forgotten bill from the couturier; with an unconquerable smile and the magic aid of a coquettish madcap creation, what is easier than to hypnotise Monsieur into signing the erst-unready cheque as though it were his greatest pleasure!'

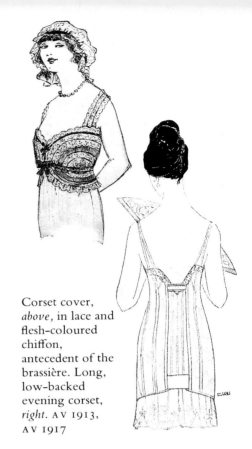

Corset cover, *above,* in lace and flesh-coloured chiffon, antecedent of the brassière. Long, low-backed evening corset, *right.* AV 1913, AV 1917

'My lady's boudoir madcap' of ninon, gay satin flowers. BV 1917

1920

A V 1909

AV 1909. *Mme Rose Lilli*

Ornate frills, ruffles, lace insertions: yet the lines of all these garments seemed austere in their new slimness. The negligee and tea gown, *opposite centre and right*, in silk mull and silk crepe, are laden with ruffles, tucks and lace edgings, the fashionable heavy embroidery in silk and gold threads. Corsets like those *opposite and above* were worn under lingerie gowns too; that *above* is old-fashioned, producing a still curvy figure, is laced right to the bottom, and worn over a long chemise. The corset *opposite* is straighter, more flexible, with a slit from hem to waist and pivot garters to allow the wearer more movement. The princess slip, *right*, was the smartest shape during the first half of the decade: fitted, square necked, here in lawn and Valenciennes.

AV 1909. *Menagh*

A V 1914

'Gowns that have their being within the intimate four walls of the home': tea gown, *above*, in old-gold satin, with a hood of cream net lace knotted on by Nattier-blue velvet bows, and an informal dinner negligee, *right,* caped in skunk-edged, jewel-embroidered net over layered charmeuse.

The 'saut de lit', *above* – a silken slip to throw over the nightgown on emerging from bed – has the draped back characteristic of contemporary lingerie, caught into the neck with beaded tassels. Another fashionable note was the layering of lace on the sleeve.

Vital elements of the bridal
trousseau: nightgowns in
various price ranges, *left,*
right and below, all with
'sprays of embroidery',
ribbon–gathered necklines.
The more expensive types
have Valenciennes and Cluny
lace trimmings, as do the
corset cover and drawers,
above.

Corset Construction

ESTER

ADJUSTO

PATENTED
U.S.A. -CANADA
ENGLAND

THE famous ADJUSTO is a thoroughly practical and hygienic reducing corset for full figure type. Note the "Adjusting Bands" a patented feature of inestimable value.

The Long Hip and Back

The long hip and back, the low bust, the *"new slight waist curve"*—these are the features of fashion for Fall. To produce these features to perfection, wear one of the smart new models of the exclusive

LYRA CORSETS

It will give you the modish lines, together with perfect grace and ease.

Model No. 3604 (like illustration)—Very smart model for slender and medium figures. Designed with low bust and extreme length from waist line down in front, side and back. Material, coutil, white. Boned with WALOHN.
Size, 18-30.   Price, $5.00.

The perfect form and lasting fit of a corset depend upon the boning of the garment. *Lyra Corsets* are boned with *Walohn*, the only reliable boning. It does not rust. It does not break. Strong yet pliable, it moulds the form into lines of grace and ease, and holds the shape of the garment perfectly.

We list only one of the many modish Fall models. We would ask you to have your merchant fit you to just the right model for your individual figure. If *Lyra Corsets* are not obtainable in your vicinity, write direct to us. Shall we send out booklet showing a variety of styles?—no charge.
OTHER NEW MODELS $5 to $15

American Lady Corset Co.

NEW YORK   **DETROIT**   **CHICAGO**

AV 1910

As the fashionable figure began to change rapidly, and women wanted more flexible foundations, patent corsets incorporating all kinds of new features appeared, such as these, *left and above.* By 1910 corsets left the bust unbolstered, but extended their hold over the abdomen and upper thigh giving the fashionable long, slim Empire line. Undergarments were streamlined, too: combined styles like that *opposite left,* in nainsook, were widely adopted. By 1918 combination garments were narrower still, in the lightest silks.

AV 1910. *Adjusto*

A V 1915 Claire Avery

B V 1917. *Madame Savigny*

This corset from 1915, *top*, is designed for dancing, with its cutaway hem and attached flouncing. That *above,* from 1917, emphasizes the hips more than the waist. Pink net with pink satin ruffles form an evening petticoat, *left,* full like the negligee, *right,* in net and chiffon.

A V 1917 Claire Avery. *Jacqueline*

B V 1916. *Redfern*

The waist-length petticoat, *above,* was the most fashionable type by 1917, this version is embroidered silk ninon trimmed with lace insertions and net ruffles. The chemise is now a mere slip of its former self, *right,* in chiffon with scalloped lace top.

Ninon camisole, *above*, with insertion lace and satin shoulder bands, to wear with waist-length petticoat under filmy overgarments. The pink crepe de chine combinations, *above,* are in the latest tailored style with waistband and back buttons.

Two corsets from 1917, *left and right,* the one in blue figured silk, the other in satin, favourite fabric for corsets. Both types are scantily boned, and give a high-waisted, slim silhouette, with attached soft bust supporters. Despite the addition of elastic inserts to many corsets, the upper thigh was still constricted.

1920

The brassière in its lightest form, tulle and ruched pink ribbon. BV 1920. *Earrieros*

Swansdown-edged dressing jacket. BV 1923

'The pursuit of slimness is one of the chief labours of the modern woman', noted *Vogue* in 1922. 'With the aid of the corsetière, the physical culturist and the non-starchy diet, shall we soon develop a race of slender, willowy women? After all, how much more enjoyment one can get out of life if one is slim and active, and excess of avoirdupois leads to inactivity and boredom. Long live the mode of slimness.' The streamlined boyish look of fashion since the war led to women wearing some of the slightest lingerie ever created. Twenties lingerie was exquisite: 'the raiment that is dearest and nearest to the heart of woman, grows each year more surpassingly lovely.'

'Corsets are literally the solid foundation on which our material happiness is based. . . . Many a gust of bad temper and unreasonableness might have been traced to . . . an uncomfortable corset which has irritated and tired its wearer.' Corsets began the decade as thigh-length, waist-high objects, with bones at the front, the flatness of the tummy being an essential fashion feature. The brassière was light, in fine chiffons, and smaller than it had ever been, leaving a gap of flesh, decently covered with a chemise, between itself and the corset. Rubber corsets were worn next to the skin, to 'promote perspiration, as this is how reduction takes place', other corsets over fine knickers. By 1923 the corset was changing fast, and *Vogue* advocated that it was wise to have as few as possible and replace them frequently. Newest shape was the combination corset incorporating the brassière: it was completely straight over the bust, in fine crepe de chine and silk tricot for the lissom, but in twill with boning for the larger lady. Silk jersey was used for the lightest: the skin-tight maillot with 'hose supporters' (a term which American *Vogue* now used to replace 'garters', while British *Vogue* began to use 'suspenders') on light satin ribbons. In 1923 and 1924 the corset was extremely unfashionable: 'it has totally disappeared, yet it would be wrong to think that the number of women who wear no corset at all, a practice which every woman would have us think she adhered to, is very large.' By 1926 curves were beginning to return to the silhouette, and the corset came back into favour. The emphasis was on suppleness, the new corsets so well cut and designed that boning was not essential. They had elastic panels, were boned only at the sides so that the hipline, the focal point, was smooth.

The extensive editorial coverage given to lingerie is not surprising, for it was exquisite in design, finish and colouring. Chemise and knickers were often made all in one, either in the shape of contemporary swimming-costumes, with legs like shorts, or with a frilled skirt which hid the attached knickers beneath. Another version had a shaped brassière attached. Colours were yellow, blue, violet, rose, jade, with gold net, cream lace, Greek banding over chiffon; black crepe de chine for daring evening wear. Waist-length petticoats were replaced by little skirts attached to the 'combinaison-culotte', decency maintained by the elasticated-leg combination, femininity

B V 1920

B V 1920

Gossamer-fine layers of the early
twenties. The black chemise, *opposite,* is
made from layer upon layer of fine
chiffon, with black lace for bodice and
hem. The double-faced satin ribbon
straps were a smart note. The
breakfast jacket, *above,* is of soft rose
velvet lined in chiffon and trimmed
with kolinsky fur, worn with a Dutch
cap of ecru net and lace, tied with silk
ribbons. Two nightgowns, *above and
below right,* with the décolleté look
that was fashionable in the twenties,
but still cut with a great deal of
breadth. The gown *above* is of
flesh-coloured chiffon over similar
coloured crepe de chine, that *below* of
exquisite lace over batiste. Both form
sets with matching sheets and pillows
to lounge on.

B V 1922 De Meyer. *Boue Soeurs*

FV 1924 Claire Avery. *Doucet*

'Although reduced to the minimum, the Parisienne's lingerie is yet more elegant in both shape and ornamentation', said French *Vogue* in 1924. Lingerie became more streamlined with each year of the twenties that passed. *Above*, long nightdress with embroidered yoke, hanging on the screen are pleated full knickers, a 'chemise-jupon' with inset lace, a long petticoat with godets from hip level. Matching short slip and corset cover, *left*, for wear under light dresses or negligees; another matching set, *right* – long-sleeved nightshirt, chemise and knickers. Smartest way to read in bed, *below*: propped up on lacy pillows wearing a bright yellow, button-up nightshirt.

FV 1924 Claire Avery. *Beer*

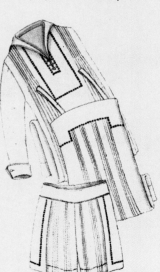

FV 1914 Claire Avery. *Beer*

FV 1923. *Beer*

BV 1920. *Stella*

'Fine linen always has its lovers, and this delightful garment [*above left*] which is a chemise and knickers combined, is also hemstitched by hand and embroidered. The nightgown [*above, second from left*] is quite short, and the front has a panel of squares made by a cross hemstitching. It is of white crepe de chine, and long-waisted. Another combination of chemise and knickers [*above right*] is also

AV 1922

in white crepe de chine, decorated with stitchery and bows of white satin ribbon. There is a camisole to match, and a crepe de chine boudoir cap trimmed with filet and Malines lace. A tucked princess petticoat [*third from left*] comes just below the knee.' The peignoir, *left*, yet another type of bedtime jacket, is of georgette crepe, trimmed with cream-coloured Margot lace, double-faced satin bows, and French rosebuds.

BV 1925 Benito

BV 1924. *Lanvin, Molyneux, Lanvin, Molyneux*

'For years women have surreptitiously been stealing men's stuff . . . pyjamas are now by far the smartest form of négligée. For a long time they have had their place in the mode, chiefly – in simple forms and washing fabrics – as a substitute for the nightgown. But recently, they have gained a new position, and one of enormous chic and popularity.' Some of the many forms of pyjama: this page, *above*, printed top in jade-greens and blues, with matching plain green trousers, *below*, four variations in shape, print and decoration. Man-tailored pyjamas, *opposite above and below*, adapted for the fair sex with lamé collar and cuffs, softly fluted neckline, in fine mousseline. Various types of pyjamas were also created for beachwear, evening wear and sportswear in addition to this lingerie version.

FV 1924

BV 1925 Benito. *Callot*

The secret of personal attractiveness

Charming natural figure lines count so much that there is a real appreciation for something that hugs, something that clings to the figure, something that makes one look slimmer at once . . . .

A V 1924. *Gossard*

The construction of corsets changed radically during the twenties. Formerly boned, heavy items, corsets were now elasticated so that they really fitted, fastenings were improved so that women could dress singlehanded, fabrics were prettier and softer. The corsets *on this page* have elastic gussets, cutaway hems for easier movement, fasten with hooks, not laces. That *above left* is all in one to give a fashionably smooth line over both bust and hips. *Opposite above* is another patent corset, designed with double front panel for fleshier women; it has a separate inner elastic vest, removable for washing. *Below left,* underwear 'tailored in the making to fit the natural lines of the figure' and, *right,* low-cut black lace camiknickers, black silk stockings.

AV 1923 Ruth Wilcox. *L. Newman & Sons*

ATHENA
UNDERWEAR
For Women and Children —and Tray-Tots for Infants

"Oh, it's all right, Marie, if it's Athena!"

AV 1924

AV 1924

BV 1928 Hoyningen-Huené. *Lanvin*

The tea gown, once 'jeune fille', frilly and demure, now emerged as a sophisticated, sexy garment: this Lanvin tea gown, *opposite*, is in pleated georgette crepe, with a silver tunic and a coat of georgette crepe bordered with silver. *Above* is a tailored pyjama outfit of heavy crepe de chine banded with silver braid. The coat, bordered by a Paisley design in white and red, achieves fullness without bulk by means of numerous narrow tucks. Three fashionable combinations, *right*, and a nightdress, all in georgette and crepe, with lace and embroidery. The combination, *near right*, has cutaway armholes to ensure its invisibility under evening gowns.

BV 1926. *Vionnet*

'Nothing is allowed which gives bulk, but there is no lack of intricate stitchery
and beautiful workmanship to relieve the simplicity of straight lines':
combinations, chemises and knickers all similarly slender. Combinations
range from the ultra-simple, *this page far left and right*, to the
petalled, *above right,* and the knicker, vest and petal skirt
dancing versions *opposite above right*. The chemise is tailored,
tucked to give shaping, the knickers trimmed down
to the minimum, too, with drawn-thread work,
lace trimmings for prettiness.

BV 1927. *Above left and below, Dickins & Jones; above right, Robinson & Cleaver, Dickins & Jones*

1930

Panelled, elasticated,
longline corset which
clung to the body.
FV 1935. *Gloriane*

Slip with built-in lastex brassière.
AV 1932 Lee Erickson. *Franklin Simon*

The clothes of the thirties were slimline, and, in contrast to those of the previous decade, cut to fit at bust, waist *and* hips. Feminine curves were back in fashion, but their extent was limited, as British *Vogue* noted in 1935: 'You can't have any bulges in your figure'. The wide range of corsets, waist-length 'girdles' and brassières available for every figure during the decade was designed to conceal such unfashionable protuberances, but their shapes did not change drastically between 1930 and 1939. The majority of corsets were full-length to achieve the smooth silhouette, particularly over the hips, focal points for most of the decade. Corsets were, thus, substantial. The introduction of woven and net elastic into lingerie in 1935 lightened the load, for this fabric could take over control from the heavy panels of batiste and brocade. 'Two-and-a-half ounces – that's the weight of the all-in-one on the scales. No more, in fact, than your pearls . . . skilful designing has banished bulk, fabrics have become light as webs, yet incredibly firm.'

Corsets were not worn merely to shape the figure. Although the idea that corseting was morally beneficial to the wearer had disappeared, great emphasis was still laid on the supportive function of lingerie. 'Women's abdominal muscles are notoriously weak,' said *Vogue* in 1932, 'and even hard exercise doesn't keep your figure from spreading if you don't give it some support.' The narrow girdles and lacy brassières of the late twenties were replaced by longer, higher, firmer corsets in the early thirties. There were special girdles and all-in-ones for the wide variety of sports now fashionable: with shorts-style legs for riding and ski-ing, without suspenders (garters), or cut away over the upper thigh for tennis and athletics. 'Uplift' became an important feature of brassières, provided by darts and circular stitching. Trimming was kept to a minimum in order to provide a smooth surface.

Major changes, however, took place in fibres and finishes for foundation garments. Until the thirties elastic was knitted on hand-knitting machines in narrow widths and short lengths. Technological developments during the decade meant that it became available in different gauges (strand sizes), and could be woven, circular-knitted or made like bobbin lace, into net, lacy designs. The entire girdle was now elasticated, like the 'roll-on', which was a seamless tube of circular-knit elastic, or a mixture of firm and elasticated fabrics, both for decorative and varied degrees of control. Lingerie was revolutionized. Foundation garments now fitted the body accurately of their own accord, without tight lacing or hooking. The zip, used for lingerie in the United States from 1931, was the most practical and popular type of fastening.

As the decade progressed, lighter and lighter girdles appeared, in silk-covered elastic net which was comfortable and attractive, particularly when lace designs were incorporated into the net. Many had firm or even boned panels at centre front, as fashion required flat stomachs. 'The variety of modern corsets is bewildering – in shape, texture, firmness, and material. Two-way elastic, woven so as to stretch both up and down and sideways, is a wonderful invention for the slim and agile, and young girls who have hitherto hated to wear corsets love it. It stretches . . . and then contracts smoothly around you.' Suddenly, in the autumn of 1939, just before war was declared in Europe, fashion tightened its belt. The waist became a focal point, encased in a new type of corset which was laced at the back from just under the bust to hip level. *Vogue* said: 'You must not let a little thing like a wasp-waist frighten you in the least. And don't let anyone picture a modern woman gasping for breath. Nowadays clever corsets ease you gently into the silhouette that used to be achieved with a coat of armour.'

Knickers, chemises (a word used now for what had been 'camiknickers'), full-length and short slips were all cut slimly, often on the bias so that they clung to the body. 'All possible ingenuity has been exerted to combine the minimum of bulk with the maximum of grace,' said *Vogue*. Different combinations of underwear were used for various occasions: 'step-in' knickers with brassière for evening, with chemise for daytime, with slip (which had a built-in brassière) for sport. Slips lengthened in keeping with skirt hems, were fitted under the arms and tucked or pleated under the bust, with flared skirts. Knickers were shorter, often yoked, and narrower than ever before. Ornamentation was kept to a minimum, to ensure that no lacy ruffles would be visible through outer garments, but, said *Vogue* in 1932, 'Too much practical lingerie makes a dull woman. An occasional frill is good for the soul.' Net and embroidery, decorative hems and seaming were popular on satin, chiffon, rayon crepe garments.

Nightgowns imitated evening gowns: in black georgette, fine silks and satins, their full skirts touched the ground, or, in lighter mood, reached mid-calf. Bodices were fitted, often low-backed, or halter-necked. Elegant and formal, these gowns played a dual role of boudoir gown and bed gown, and could be dressed up with fashionable boleros and tiny bedjackets to be worn for intimate dinners, within the house.

Lingerie colours in the early thirties were pastel: flesh, all the pinks, ivory, pale blues and greens. Darker colours became popular later in the decade: rich burgundies and reds, black. Earlier, fabrics for corsets and brassières were batiste, satin, net, crepe de chine, linen, poplin; later, plain or patterned elastic net, elasticated satin, matt silk and rayon. Other lingerie items were made from fabrics soft enough to drape, to stretch on the bias: crepe-backed satin, crepe de chine, fine tulle, chiffon, printed ninon, mousseline, glove silk, shantung. At the end of the decade there was a revival of hand-stitched lingerie with lace and rolled hems, to be worn over the laced, wasp-waisted corset. Once more made from the batistes and heavy cottons used earlier in the century, it 'sealed the victory of the corset over your shape.'

Slim, yoked knickers in ninon and Alençon lace. A V 1934. *Jay-Thorpe*

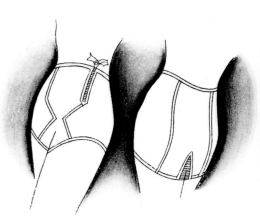

Riding corset: cut away but controlled, newly zip fastened. F V 1936. *Gloriane*

1940

Nightgowns cut on evening lines, in chiffon and georgette, bare the arms and even the back, sweep down to the ground. A V 1937 Giorgio de Chirico. *Bonwit Teller (1, 3), Saks-Fifth Avenue (2), Bergdorf Goodman (4, 5)*

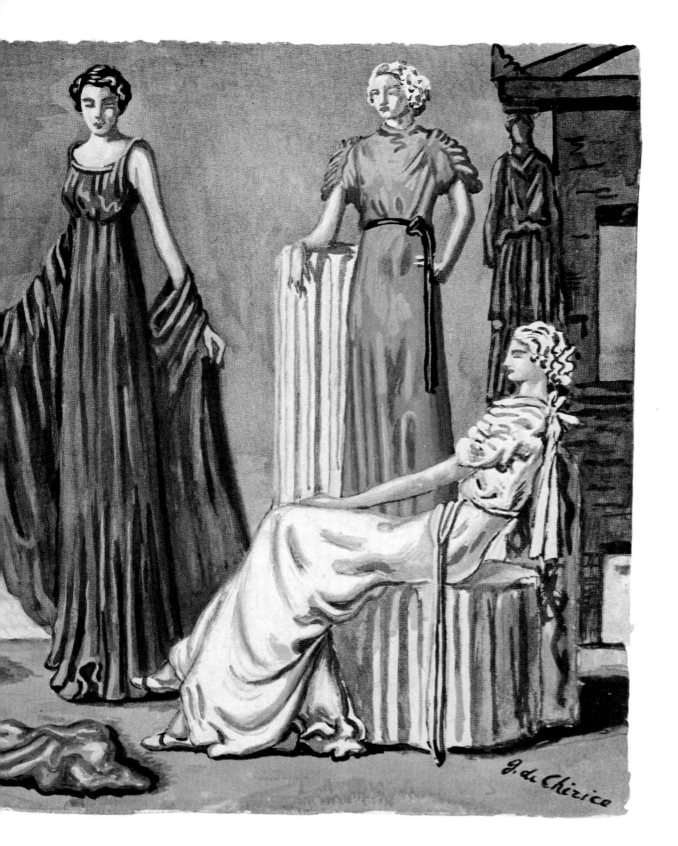

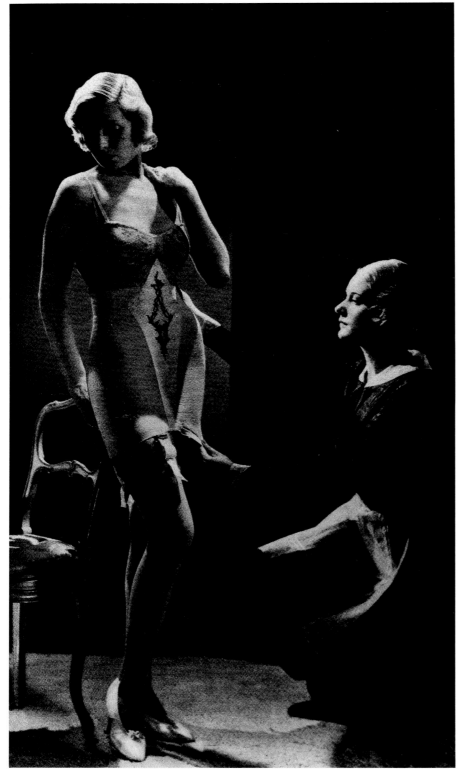

AV 1937 Steichen. *American Lady*

BV 1932 Horst

'The modern choice, between separate belt and brassière and all-in-one corsets, is divided . . . but for evening the all-in-one is best'. Two examples, *left and above,* with the fashionable smooth line from bust to thigh; there were various ways of cutting the corset over the diaphragm, to flatten the tummy. The earlier style, *left,* has a decorative padded brassière section, but by 1937 the shaped 'uplift' brassière, *above,* had become popular. Both corsets use the new 'lastex' elastic yarn. Nightgowns (*opposite*) reach to mid-calf or further, their slender lines ornamented only with light embroidery and tucking, echoing dresses. The lace-edged bolero, *opposite left,* was a smart addition.

1931. *F. Lippé, Annek, Charlotte Paquet*

Caryatids in corsets, *left*. The majority make use of the wide range of elasticated fabrics available, the finest of which, hand-loomed silk chiffon elastic, makes the strapless evening corset, *near left*. Brassières are smaller, the the cups seamed for better fit. Lacing, absent from the smartest lingerie for a decade, has made its reappearance in the side-laced corset, *centre*, and in the back-laced, boned style *second from right*. More Hellenic beauties, *below*, carved in soap and clad, sylph-like, in two-way stretch corsets.

AV 1934. *Carter's*

AV 1939 De Molas. *Munsingwear, Bonwit Teller, Warner Brothers, Lily of France, Cadolle*

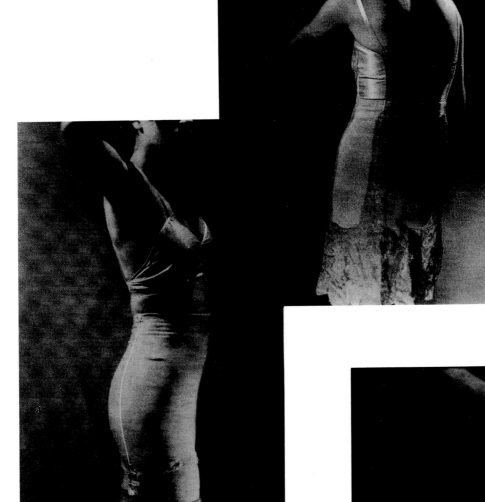

The changing mood in lingerie photography and design. *On this page* (*left*) an all-in-one girdle and brassière, still lightly boned and high-waisted. The slip is fitted, heavily ornamented with lace. During the decade the waistline returned to its natural position, lingerie clung more tightly to the body, emphasizing the hips, as elasticated fabrics were used. Suddenly, in late 1939, the waist became the focal point of fashion, encased in a new breed of laced, unyielding corsets like the 'detolle' model, *opposite*, which reached from just below the bust to hip level.

B V 1930 Steichen

1940

All-in-one sheath of rayon jersey for a bulkless fit. A V 1943 Rawlings. *Kayser*

The forties were a time of great change in fashion as a whole. For lingerie it was a decade of strong contrasts: some of the dullest, and some of the most exciting lingerie of the century. Dull, because the erotic corsets that had stunned the fashion world in 1939, nipping the waist and emphasizing the bust, temporarily disappeared when war broke out and were replaced by simple, functional garments. The finest corsetry elastic had been hand-loomed in France, and many fabrics had been woven there too, so after the outbreak of war lingerie had to adapt itself to new fibres and clumsier construction. As British *Vogue* noted, there was 'no lace; no embroidery, no frills; but any amount of elegance in the new lingerie', the 'elegance' being contained in the way it was worn. Far more significant for the evolution of lingerie was the development of nylon. An unknown quantity to the general public when its discovery was announced by Du Pont in 1938, excitement mounted during the decade as the full potential of the fibre began to be realized. It was not until well after the war that nylon became available outside the United States as a fashion fibre, and when it did it was extremely expensive, almost twice the price of rayon. The fibre had many advantages: it was strong, light, supple, could be woven or knitted by machine, was available in various deniers (weights) for different lingerie functions, it washed very easily, dripped dry and needed little or no ironing.

The hourglass figure, although it disappeared from European styles as soon as the war broke out, lasted until mid-war in the United States. It was replaced in both continents by what American *Vogue* described as 'The Greek idea in fashion . . . the free supple lines . . . freedom from constraint . . . beautiful cut and drape of fabrics over a naturally curved figure.' Rationing of food probably made the corset's job less demanding; there was, in any case, less room for growth in the wartime type of corset, which was usually made from a combination of firm cotton, shantung or rayon and narrow elastic panels. Some American versions used nylon net. The bust was emphasized by wartime clothes, aided by the increasingly well-cut brassière. Where twenty years earlier this garment had been two darted pieces of fabric, it was now carefully cut and seamed for a variety of figure types, and often boned or underwired to give the breasts a more substantial silhouette. After the war the bosom continued to be a focal point of fashion, as American *Vogue* noted in 1946: 'In Paris the figure is in fashion. The nipped-in waist, the rounded bosom are what they asked of a figure. And now Paris has inventions for just *that*.' British *Vogue*, mindful of the Board of Trade sartorial restrictions, was less enthusiastic: 'There are moments when fashion changes fundamentally . . . this is one of those moments. Granted that we in England will not partake of it very far or very fast, at present'. The 'guimpe', or 'guêpière', and the 'waspie' were the corsets created by the Couturiers as foundations for the new lines and were later adapted by the lingerie companies for mass-production. 'Femininity' crept back into fashion. By 1948 the waspie no longer reached from breast to hip, with firm boning: it was now called the 'waist-liner' and was only some eight inches deep, in nylon net and elastic. Girdles and brassières were increasingly flexible, as after the war women began once again to play tennis, ride, ski; brassière backs were elasticated, straps too, sizings were improved to take account not only of the chest measurement but also of the size of the breasts. It was now necessary to own a selection of lingerie for various shapes: 'current fashions, requiring a smooth continuity between rounded bosom, curved-in waistline and rounded hips, have resulted in corsets being considered in relation to clothes as well as to individual measurements.'

'Simplification is a twentieth-century word,' said American *Vogue* in 1943, 'it belongs to lingerie, to these bare essentials.' American lingerie had begun the decade in a far prettier way than European equivalents, with lace insets, hand-stitching, the garments cut more widely, usually on the bias unless in jersey. By mid-war this had changed, all lingerie was now cut for practicality, swiftness in manufacture. Pre-war lace stocks had run out, and even machine embroidery was a luxury. Knickers were small, cut away at the front or sides over the upper thigh for ease of movement, and some had elasticated sides, thus combining the roles of knicker and corset. Petticoats were knee length, slimly cut with brassière- or camisole-shaped top. War-time nightwear was simple too. No longer did nightgowns resemble evening gowns, they were demure, girlish shapes, with high necks, or cut like petticoats. American styles were 'shirred to extol the bosom', and were less austere in trimming and styling. Housecoats were rather masculine, with shoulder pads, turnback collars and tie waists. But recovery was swift. American *Vogue* noted in 1946 that: 'After the austere years of unpretty lingerie we can have it once again frilled and be-ribboned in the feminine way.' Slips acquired lace bodices with satin ribbons; they imitated the lines of the frocks worn over them. Some corsets acquired frilly 'petticoats' attached to them, providing an all-in-one for evening wear. Knickers were cut on the bias, or made from jerseys for even better fit. Nightgowns were frilled and appliquéd with lace. Sleeves were important: some were puffed, in wide bell shapes or later long, full, gathered at the wrist.

Silk was still a popular fabric in the more expensive ranges of lingerie, but rayon was most widely used until the advent of nylon. Brassières and girdles were made from all the elasticated fabrics (such as silk), also from firm fabrics like cotton, shantung, net, satin, brocade, later from nylon in all its forms: power net, taffeta, satin, chiffon, mesh. Other lingerie items transferred their allegiance, too, from rayon and cotton to nylon. 'Frills, laces and longer-than-wrist-length sleeves' said *Vogue* 'add up importantly – topped perhaps with a narrow white ribbon and smooth-brushed hair'.

Dior's New Look underbodice, curving the bust and hips. BV 1947 Coffin. *Christian Dior*

The waistliner, here built into a petticoat. AV 1948 Rutledge. *Colura*

1950

'In Paris, the figure
is in fashion'. One
of the earliest
waist-nipping
corsets to return to
fashion after the
war, *opposite*, a
boned waistband to
strap on like a belt,
gave even thin girls
contours. Two
years later appeared
this type, *left*, in
nylon marquisette
and elastic, much
lighter and unboned
with built-in
brassière. BV 1946
Horst. *Piquet*
(*opposite*); AV 1948
Horst. *La Trique*
(*left*)

A V 1924 R. R. Bouché. *This page, Patricia; opposite, Flexees, Le Gant, Lily of France, Poirette*

BV 1949 John Ward.
Illa Knina, Macmillan
and Dowidat

On previous page: American slips and nightgowns, *left*, in rayon are frilly and fuller than European types. As light and supple as the ballerinas, the corsets, *right,* are entirely of nylon, seamed to emphasize the bust and slender torso.

'A figure's not-God-given grace depends on good exercise, good corseting. The exercise is up to will power; the corset to wise choice.' Evening styles, *opposite:* far left is a girdle for the Empire line, reaching almost to the strapless, décolleté broderie anglaise brassière. Designed for firm control, it has elastic satin side panels, back lacing. The evening corselette next to it is in black lace over white satin with underwired brassière and back lacing. *On this page* is a very flexible girdle made from elasticated fabric, with a small centre-front satin panel, for daytime wear.

A V 1946 R. R. Bouché.
Tru Balance

Stroboscopic
photograph,
opposite,
demonstrates the
stretch of the corset
in rayon satin and
elastic net, under
nylon lace-trimmed
negligee with the
fashionable frilly
sleeve emphasis. *On
this page*, posed
against a panel of
details borrowed
from French steel
engravings, the
'ancien régime'
look in gathered
rayon satin,
betraying its
hellenic origins.

A V 1944 Gjon Mili
A V 1944 Kay Bell

The demure negligee, *opposite left*, with high neck and long sleeves, was high fashion at the end of the war. The slip, *opposite right*, contemporary with the negligee, is slenderly cut, has no ornament but a dash of nylon chiffon around the hem. By 1948 lingerie was once more lacy, and fuller, as the silk chemise (now another name for camiknickers) and petticoat *on this page* demonstrate.

A V 1948 Horst.
Odette Barsa

1950

Permanently pleated nylon, popular for all lingerie, in an Empire line nightdress. B V 1954. *The White House*

'This is the new figure,' said *Vogue* in 1950, 'the body line beneath the new mid-century fashions. You see an unexaggerated bosom, a concave middle, a close hipline, a seemingly long leg . . . the same figure that might have been successfully squeezed at the waistline and freed to curve at the hips, last year, can be taught to conform to the new line.' Throughout the decade, the body's natural shape was mercilessly moulded into a variety of shapes, choice of which depended on time of day, but still more on the fashionable lines adopted by individual designers. The overall look was an overtly sexy one; it was full of sharp outlines in breasts, narrow torso, sloping hips: aggressively female rather than softly feminine. Developments in lingerie were less radical than in the preceding decade, revolving around new uses of nylon, such as permanent pleating, the production of still lighter elastic nets, better-engineered strapless brassières, smoother silhouettes. *Vogue* emphasized the benefits of a good diet and plenty of exercise, in addition to good corseting, for the attainment of the ideal figure. Nightwear was newly full and frilly, with billows of nylon, cottons or silks, all lavishly trimmed.

During the first years of the fifties the Couture houses continued to commission lingerie designs (some even produced their own styles) to provide a foundation for their fashion 'lines'. Later in the decade this link lessened, as the lingerie companies began to set their own trends too, albeit more in finish and fabric than in silhouette. The waist was still small: 'Whatever caprices fashion may adopt, the waist will not let go of its newly refound slenderness so soon', noted French *Vogue* in 1950. Indeed the waist remained slim (not as radically so as in the late forties) throughout the decade. Girdles assisted it in this aim, extending over the torso and almost reaching the brassière. The all-in-one was still very popular, particularly suitable for those with 'spare-tyre trouble': it helped to give a smoother silhouette. By 1953 the smartest silhouettes had just a suspicion of a tummy, firmly controlled bottom and a no longer 'unexaggerated' bosom. Breast size was becoming important, lingerie companies produced styles with foam rubber and plastic inserts, wadding, spiral stitching and clever shaping to increase the bosom, and to raise, separate and round the breasts. Their natural shape was not a matter of interest to the fashion world until the following decade. 'Every woman who's reached the age of fashion-reason knows it: her figure's as contemporary as her corsetry', said *Vogue* in 1955, as the higher bust and waist lines demanded change in foundations. By the end of the decade corsets were still more streamlined, with attached petticoats in layers of lace for evening wear, the corset itself often made from black or white lace lined with pastel coloured voile. Brassières and all-in-ones were lighter, often strapless for added freedom. Pantie-girdles like shorts, reaching the knee, were new; they smoothed away bulges made visible by the fashion for tight blue-jeans and slacks. The silhouette was the important thing, the proportions of the body beneath quite irrelevant, so long as it could be squeezed, padded out and elastic-coated into the accepted shape.

Chemises (camiknickers) and slips were slim and elegant, knee-length, their bodices and hems trimmed with nylon lace, pleated nylon tulle, or ruffles. Waist-length petticoats were worn beneath full skirts, in printed voile or jersey, their colours soft enough not to show through. Combination foundations, incorporating brassière, girdle, petticoat and knickers were popular in the late fifties. At this time too, there were silks and cottons for lingerie, in addition to nylon in its many forms. Nightwear began the decade on the same slim lines as the rest of lingerie, but soon filled out, became lighthearted and frilly. 'All volume, no weight' was the rule for nightdresses and dressing gowns which, at their most luxurious, were made from sheerest voile and chiffons. Sleeveless or handkerchief-sleeved gowns had low, ruffled, round necks or high yoked bodices; some were waisted, all belled out into a full skirt. Over them were worn full dressing gowns, to complete the négligé, which were still more ruffled, often tied with ribbons to match those in the hair. Colours were pastel: peach, turquoise, azure, pink or white with coloured ribbons. Pleating remained fashionable throughout the first half of the decade; by mid-decade stripes and flower prints, still in pastels, had invaded the bedroom. Gowns 'can be knee high', said *Vogue*, 'or they can sweep the floor; that's the newly arrived alternative. Short dressing-gowns, young and very modern, might have been made for travelling.' Bedjackets, too, had shrunk to bolero size, with narrow collars and elbow-length sleeves. This sleeve length, whether bell-shaped, or gathered into a huge puff, became the most popular, particularly with yoked negligees, which swirled out from masses of tiny gathers to the knee. The high waist which invaded daytime clothes in 1958 affected lingerie the following year.

Nylon was still the infant prodigy of the textile trade, particularly for lingerie, as *Vogue* noted, 'because of its famous lightness and speed in drying, and because it is now so enchantingly pretty'. In tricot, Chantilly-type lace, crepe, net, crepe de chine, taffeta, voile, permanently pleated or combined with elastic, it was extremely versatile. For most of the decade it was *the* lingerie fibre, although cotton and silk made a strong bid for supremacy in their lightest, embroidered forms. Foundation garments were made from nylon: ninon, poplin, lace, broche batiste, net. Elasticated fabrics – nylon lace-patterned elastic net, elasticated satin – grew ever lighter and were used for complete foundation garments, with minimum seaming, in their finest forms. Corsets, if not the seamless 'roll-on' type, were usually fastened with zips. Embroidery, lace, net edgings and frillings, ribbon trimmings abounded. Coloured lingerie, in coffee, tea rose, turquoise, coral, pinks, peach, soft flower prints and candy stripes, was popular for most of the decade. Finally there was a revival of whitest white.

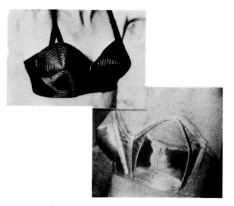

Whirlpool stitched brassière *above*, boned, strapless satin type *below*. BV 1953 Patrick Matthews. *Florelle, Demoiselle*

The concave silhouette. BV 1953 Frances McLaughlin. *Lefaucheur/ Christian Dior*

1960

'The body line beneath mid-century fashions.' The waistline is still small, held in by a long-line girdle in peach-coloured satin and 'Youthlastic', the breasts encased in a structured, poplin brassière. The cut of clothes, placing bulk above the waist and thus attenuating the line below, depended on well-cut lingerie to provide the right foundation.

B V 1950 Blumenfeld. *Warner, Jacques Fath*

◢ 1953 Robert Randall.
andide

A wisp of silk mousseline to
wake up in, *opposite*, with
high waist, very low, ruffled
neckline. Puffed and gathered
sleeves, whether short, as
here, or elbow length as *on
this page,* were very popular
for nightgowns and negligees.
The wide-yoked neckline of
the housecoat imitates the
fashionable décolletage; pastel
tones, stripes and flower
prints were a mid-decade
mode.

BV 1954 Parkinson.
Horrockses

FV 1959 Willy Rizzo.
Kayser

Layers and layers of
nylon, *on this page*
and *opposite right,*
make ultra-feminine
nightwear; lace
billows down the
front of the gown,
opposite right, from
neck to hem, nylon
frills edge the full
gown *on this page.*
The layered,
hooded gown
opposite left is made
from embroidered
cotton, which had
returned once more
to popularity.

Opposite left FV 1959
Willy Rizzo. *Silhouette*
Opposite right FV 1959
Willy Rizzo

A V 1956 Karen Radkai. *Givenchy for Jantzen*

'Lingerie colours that are intensely colourful, rather than *rather* colourful'. Sapphire-blue foundation, *above,* which makes the skin look like alabaster. Panelled in nylon lace, satin, net, with lastex back section, it provides firm control, like the peach Dacron and nylon corset *opposite,* which slips on like a stocking, has no fastenings. High-waisted slip to match the corset, *right,* is polished to a long, smooth line, set in a deep edging of nylon lace.

V 1956 Eric. *Warners, Vanity Fair*

1959 Don Honeyman.
iumph

Lingerie secrets revealed, *this page and opposite*. The pantie-girdle has decreased in coverage during the decade: no longer does it extend over the torso, or over the upper thigh, but is briefer and more flexible. Strapless bras were popular throughout the decade, this underwired version is in Perlon taffeta and lace. The fashion for narrow blue-jeans and slacks created the need for slenderizing lingerie beneath them. The girdle is in lightweight elastic net, with double panel over the tummy, and is invisible under clothes.

FV 1959 Meerson. *Fairbell*

1960

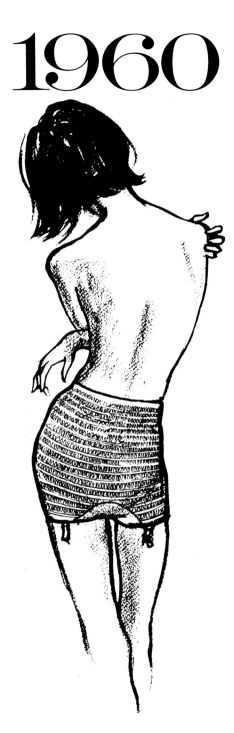

'New fundamental fashion is flowing in a fluid line, light and alive . . . naturally shaped', said *Vogue* in 1968. The exaggerated curves of the fifties, achieved with boning, padding, underwiring and firm corseting, gradually disappeared. In their place returned the natural curves, smoothed and controlled with light, elastic lingerie. The fashionable figure changed from bosomy and narrow waisted to a tall, slim, boyish shape: even Haute Couture became aware of teenage requests for fashions designed for their age group. From this time fashion aimed at women in their teens and early twenties, rather than at women some ten years senior. Clothes were light-hearted, changing in look from season to season, even from day to day. Lingerie had to be simple and versatile, brief, too, for many clothes were décolleté, very short, with cut-out designs, bare midriffs. The miniskirt, which made instant fashion news in the mid-sixties, had a profound effect on lingerie: stocking-tops were visible, and tights gradually became the most-worn leg covering. Bikini briefs replaced larger and looser types. But the new lightness in clothes was not only aesthetic, nor merely a result of fashion's newly acquired youth: a new group of fibres, elastomerics (renamed elastane in 1976) had actually reduced lingerie weight. 'A little vanity, a little will-power – and only an ounce or two of Lycra or Vyrene [alternative names for the miracle fibre, Spandex] will make you a lighter woman,' said *Vogue*. Lycra had all the properties of elastic – with the addition of resistance to abrasion, perspiration and damage by detergents and lotions – and could be knitted in its raw state. It was three times as powerful, weight for weight, as elastic, removing the need for boning in corsetry.

At the outset of the sixties corsets were firm, strapless or sold with detachable straps, décolleté, hip length. Girdles were less rigid, in sections of embroidered nylon, or Helanca lace and Spandex or elastic. The two-way pull style, with panels of elastication crossing in an X over the stomach, was highly popular. Bras were padded, often underwired, giving a rounded, but artificial, silhouette. The arrival of Spandex catalysed the youthful mood: lingerie became lighter and more flexible. For the young there were matching sets of bra, suspender (garter) belt and bikini briefs in nylon lace. Later versions were bra and briefs in nylon tricot, which gave little support, the suspender belt (beginning to disappear in favour of tights) in matching nylon, often printed. For those needing more support there were briefer girdles, some of which did not even reach the waist now that hipster clothes were fashionable, in Lycra and lace; with minimal seaming and boning. Pantie-girdles had a back trouser seam to give a rounded natural effect.

Bras, in embroidered nylon, cotton, lace, net, were light, with some padding in the cups. By the end of the decade cups had become softer, revealing the natural shape of the breasts: 'Bosoms become more rounded as bras lose that pre-formed pointed look' said *Vogue*. Nylons with no elastic

Ultra light pantie-girdle with suspenders (garters), in Ban-Lon. F V 1961 Hervé Dubly. *Teenform*

stretch were used for bra cups, mounted on elastic to fit snugly around the ribs, straps were made from polypropylene which did not twist or roll up, and were worn either straight over the shoulders, or crossed over at the back for added support. 'Drive, jump, ride, stretch, accelerate into spring with briefer, simpler foundations, that you can put on and forget . . . they look like you, move like you, feel like you', said *Vogue* in 1968. Flower prints, spots, splashes of colour adorned the newest, youngest lingerie. At the end of the sixties bodystockings were worn under the fashionable crocheted dresses and clinging and transparent clothes, giving little support in Bri-nylon, more in Lycra, particularly in the briefly fashionable foundation that extended from shoulders to ankle. The long corselette was revived for day and evening, wired and elasticated; a new breed of waist-cinchers, reaching down to hip-level this time, smoothed larger silhouettes.

Matching sets of lingerie were popular throughout the sixties: 'bra to slip to belt, the lace trimmings and panel insets match perfectly throughout the set', noted *Vogue*. Lingerie was slighter, less was worn. Slips were shorter – mere scraps of printed nylon elasticated at the waist. The few long versions had underwired bras incorporated into the design, but their popularity was short-lived, the demand being for lighter garments. Briefs were tiny (but knee-length bloomers were a passing craze), all in nylon and elastomerics, bright, printed, even in paper during the paper clothes craze mid-decade. As tights appeared in one of their earliest forms, stockings attached to panties, sales of panties decreased.

Nylon nightdresses were replaced by cotton and Terylene blends, nylon and cotton, Dacron, which looked like freshly ironed cotton, but needed little ironing. Others were silk and wool mix, crepe for nightdresses, chiffons and georgettes for matching peignoirs. The long, slim, square-necked nightdress was upstaged by 'baby dolls', which *Vogue* described as 'little cotton shorts-suits lightly frilled and ruffled . . . the prettiest cool new nightdressing.' They had lacy necklines like camisoles, or were gathered. In spotted cotton, broderie anglaise, Indian and jazzy prints, with ribbons and bows, even worn without briefs, the mini-nightie was high fashion.

New fibres and manufacturing processes shaped lingerie. Foundation garments were made from the elastomerics, both in net and woven with other fibres to produce lacy, matt surfaces, from embroidered nylon, straps from polypropylene. Briefs were made from nylon knit, cotton knits, cotton and nylon mixes, slips from nylon lace, jersey, cottons, Dacron and cotton mix, voile, dotted swiss. Most popular nightdress fabrics were cotton look-alikes, silk, wool and chiffon. Complete lingerie outfits, underwear and nightwear, were co-ordinated with matching prints, appliqués, or cutouts. Plain colours were later supplemented by psychedelic prints: 'New under-fashions', said *Vogue*, 'have a pulse-beat brilliance.'

Mini-nightie with lace frilling. F V 1967 Arnaud de Rosnay. *Pierre Cardin*

Quant's first lingerie. B V 1965 Norman Parkinson. *Mary Quant*

1970

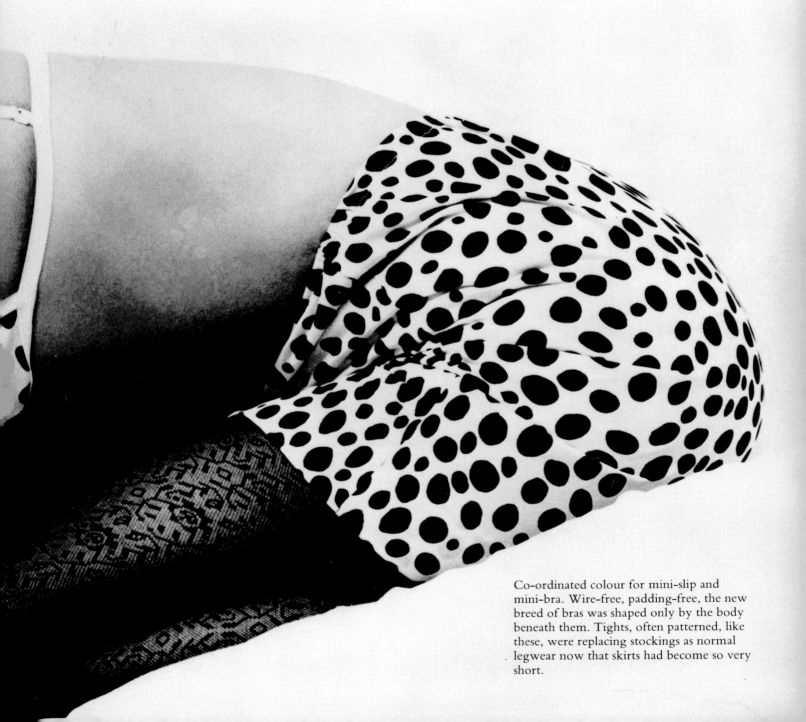

BV 1967 Helmut Newton.
Rudi Gernreich for Exquisite Form
(bra and slip) *Balenciaga* (tights)

Co-ordinated colour for mini-slip and
mini-bra. Wire-free, padding-free, the new
breed of bras was shaped only by the body
beneath them. Tights, often patterned, like
these, were replacing stockings as normal
legwear now that skirts had become so very
short.

V 1965 Guy Bourdin.
Vanity Fair

The shapes of the early
sixties on show: they
changed radically during
the first five years. The
brassière and girdle *on this
page* still resemble fifties
lingerie: the girdle,
although shrinking in
depth, is still heavy, the
brassière spiral-stitched,
padded, thus hiding the
shape of the breasts
beneath. Both are made
from Helanca nylon lace,
marquisette, elastic net.
The later brassière and
pantie-girdle, *opposite*,
reveal and contour the
body's natural shape, the
brassière in light nylon
tricot, the girdle in Lycra.

B V 1962 Irving Penn.
Hollywood Vassarette

FV 1967 Jeanloup Sieff. *Formfit*

Lightest bra yet, for the slender, *above*, in
nylon and elastic. The straps were adjustable
for wear as here or as a halter neck, seaming
subtly shaped and almost invisible in wear.
Corselettes, *right*, in close contact with the
fashion machine (Hawkins slimming
machines in fact), cut for wear with tights,
in light, firm Lycra to shape the
less-than-sylphlike. Both have minimally
padded bras, adjustable straps; that *above* is in
white Lycra with piped stripes of tangerines
and blues, that *below* is patterned with pink
and green flowers on white, has a low-cut
V back.

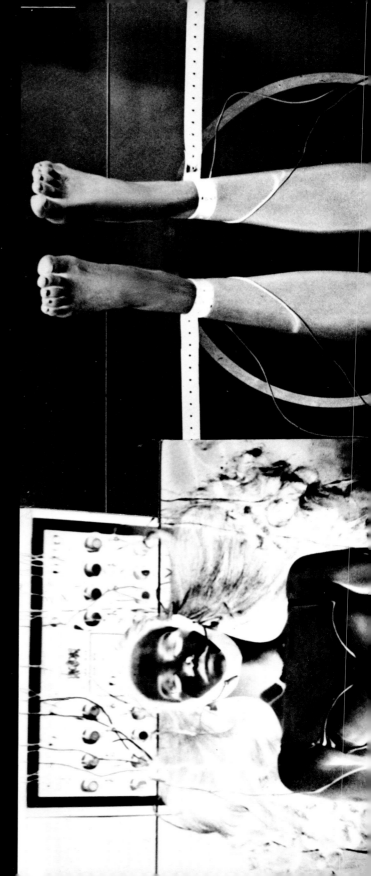

BV 1968 Helmut Newton.
Lovable (above), Flexees (below)

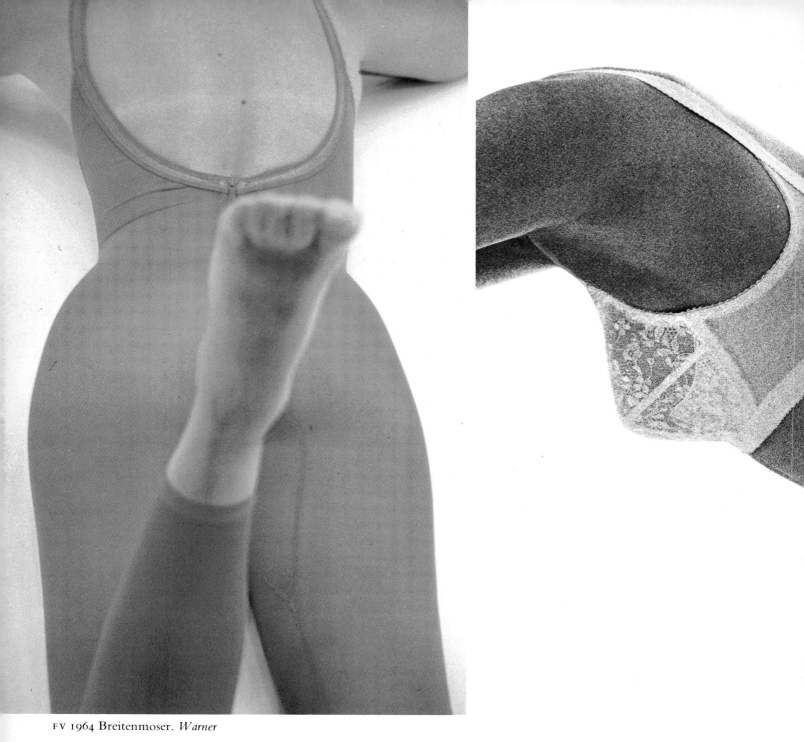

FV 1964 Breitenmoser. *Warner*

Total control: Lycra foundation garment, *above,* to contour the body
from shoulder to ankle. Less extensive, but equally light and lively are the
girdles and bras, *right,* designed to cope with most figure problems, to be
worn with either stockings or tights.

BV 1967 Peter Rand. *Main picture and inset 3rd from left: Mademoiselle
Sarongster* (bra), *Playtex* (girdle); *others, from left to right: Berlei,
Silhouette, J. S. Blair*

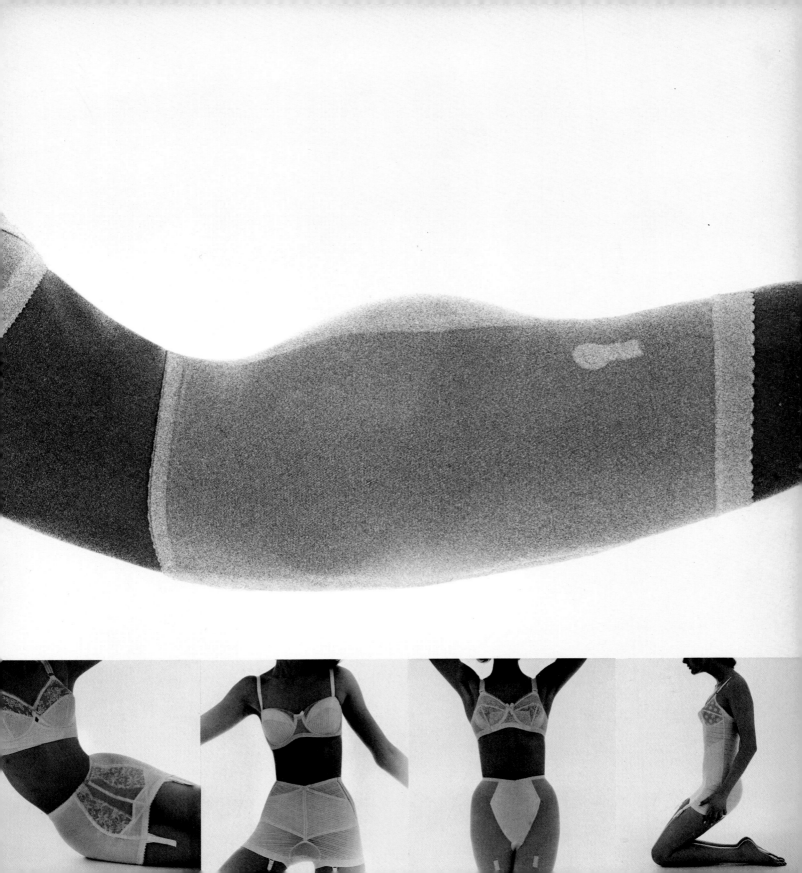

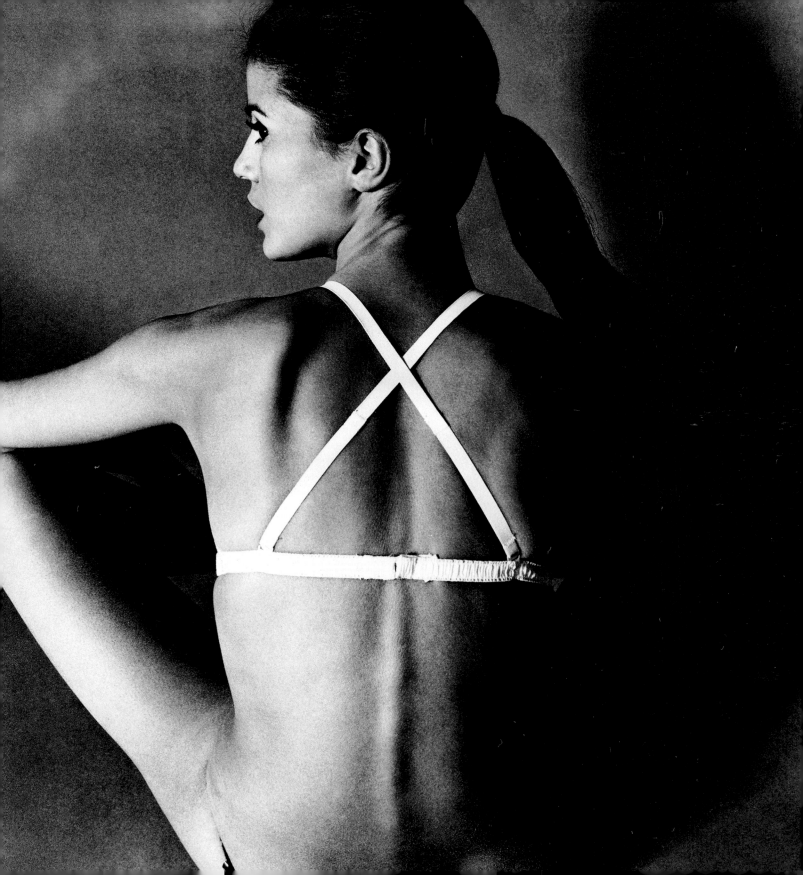

On previous page: hipster fashions provoked the rejuvenation of the midriff-cinching corset, *left*, here in lace and black nylon, providing a smooth curve from bust to hip. Supple, sporty bra, *right,* with stretchy crossover straps for extra support.

FV 1967 Guy Bourdin. *Lady Marlene*
BV 1967 Guy Bourdin. *Warners*

Flower power lingerie, *this page and opposite.* Firm control girdle, *opposite,* has extra-strength stitching at the front, those *on this page* range from firm to minimum control, all are in Lycra. The bras, in nylon and nylon tricot are printed to team, most are underwired, lightly padded.

AV 1968 Alexis Waldeck. *Vanity Fair, Rudi Gernreich* (tights)
BV 1968 Philip Castle. *Warners, Berlei, Lovable*

1970

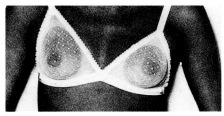

Moulded Lycra and nylon bra. BV 1975 Peccinotti. *Marks and Spencer*

Barely-there bra and pants in silk chiffon and satin. IV 1979 Claus Wickrath. *Italbust, Malerba*

'This winter's bras no longer hide anything. As transparent as they are light, they allow the breast to remain its natural shape. Even the edges of the cups are moulding, elastic', said *Vogue* in 1970. Lingerie was ready for action: supple, diminutive, practical, uncluttered. This was fashion's mood, as every kind of exercise became fashionable and acquired its own clothing. Women wore fewer lingerie layers. The petticoat went out of fashion, bras were not obligatory, sales of panties dropped, nightwear was no longer of primary importance. Lingerie had reached its lowest ebb and its simplest shape. But the tide turned during the latter part of the seventies. A new process had been discovered whereby the curved parts of bras and girdles could be moulded seamlessly, from one piece of elastane. The look achieved was the most natural yet; it was immediately popular, particularly for bras. Girdles did not return to high fashion, but were worn by the less-than-supple. Fashion was growing up and a new mood was becoming evident as clothes emphasized the body's shape in a more sensual manner: the ingénue disappeared in favour of her wiser, if very little older, sister. Silk (and silk-look) lingerie returned in nostalgic camisoles, peignoirs, all richly edged with lace.

Bras and briefs closely resembled the bikinis in fashion. Briefs were *brief*, often with little more than a narrow rouleau or tie at the sides, holding front and back together. They were plain or patterned, in nylon and cotton jerseys, matt cottons, edged with lace. Bras had triangular, rather than rounded, cups, again in jerseys, but also in transparent matt fabrics with very little or no padding. Some had appliqué shapes in fabric or lace, most had low cleavages, very narrow back and shoulder straps. One very stretchy, comfortable type of bra was a 'mini-vest': with wide straps built into the design, it was darted in at the bust and edged with elastic lace to hold it in place. Mid-decade the rounded bra returned, with wiring to hold its very cutaway cups in place. It was still light and transparent – in glossy moulded jerseys and satins, later in crepe de chine, mousseline, georgette. Girdles, even pantie-girdles, were unfashionable. Fitness was an essential, and girdles were seen as the symbol of just the opposite, so even when moulded elastane improved the silhouette given by girdles, they did not return to high fashion. Bodystockings were followed by leotards and footless tights, stolen from the dancing world, worn as underwear or overwear. At the end of the seventies there was a revival of lacy, transparent corsets worn in bedroom and boudoir, just for fun. They acquired a practical function as the eighties approached, as décolleté, very grand evening dresses, requiring such under-pinning, swept into fashion. Silks and satins returned, too: bras and knickers were made from silky wisps edged with lace, and French knickers reappeared. There were suspender (garter) belts, too, in an attempt to rejuvenate stockings, which was largely unsuccessful.

The petticoats worn during the early seventies reached from waist to knee and were elasticated at the waist. Usually in matching sets with bra and knickers, they were made from printed cottons, printed nylon, broderie anglaise or lace. A brief-lived fashion was for knee-length frilly bloomers or petticoats to peep from beneath skirts. The slip was then discarded until the end of the decade when it returned, full-length, in silky fabrics.

Nightwear was very varied during the seventies. Many women simply discarded it altogether. The frilly 'baby dolls' of the late sixties vanished without trace, were replaced by long, soft, jersey or chiffon nightdresses, plain or printed, often with an old-world flavour. Some women adopted a more unisex look: 'Think of yourself in a rough, soft, warm pair of men's pyjamas', said *Vogue* in 1974. Pyjamas were popular in silk, cotton, wool and cotton mixes, later in fine cotton jersey, silk jersey. Towards the end of the decade silk camisoles, French knickers, even petticoats and camiknickers, were adopted for nightwear. Peignoirs, reminiscent of the bedjackets of the twenties, were made from silks edged with lace, or entirely from lace. Some young designers began to concentrate on soft lingerie in silk and lace, to produce well-cut, beautiful lingerie with a hand-finished appearance.

Lingerie colours at the beginning of the seventies were tranquil by comparison with their recent forbears. White, flesh, coffee, black with pinky mauves were the most popular. Prints were no longer popular for underwear, but contrast-coloured embroidery, particularly around motifs, was usual. Later, more adventurous colours returned: burnt orange, turquoise, fuschia, peach, apricot, pastel blues, olive green, with coffee, cream or white lace perhaps even with threaded ribbons too. Fabrics for bras increased in number during the decade. Nylon, in plain or printed jersey, or in its many non-stretch forms ranging from transparent to opaque, cotton jersey, broderie anglaise, Lycra, lace, were supplemented by net, lace and mesh, moulded Lycras, silk and silk-look satin, crepe de chine, georgette. Polyester imitations of silk had become very convincing in appearance and in feel, and could be printed with as much definition as silk. Fine cottons, too, were used. Briefs were popular in nylon jersey, in cotton jersey, broderie anglaise, lawn, cotton and polyester mixes, lace, Lycra, towelling. Petticoats and nightwear used fine cottons and cotton mixes with polyesters or wool, man-made and silk jerseys, matt and shiny silk and silk-effect fabrics, broadloom lace. All lingerie was lacy by the end of the seventies, in body or trimming, and was often subtly embroidered.

The early eighties gave a tailored edge to the sexy, feminine clothes of the late seventies. The soft, draping styles and fabrics remained, but were more closely cut. As the exercise craze died down, and fewer fashionable women were to be seen jogging in the parks at 6 a.m., lingerie which controlled excess inches seemed ripe for rejuvenation.

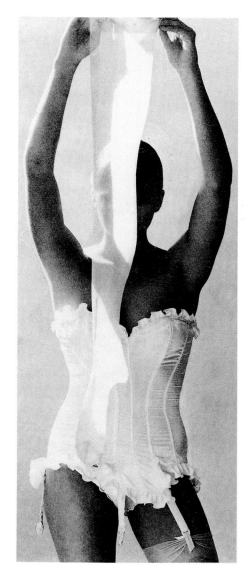

Fine, frilly corset, revived in eighties style. G V 1980 Eric Boman. *Chantal Thomass*

1980

BV 1974 Arthur Elgort. *Viyella, Rowes* (boys)

Practical nightdressing for the whole family, *above*, in stripy unisex pyjamas which were warm and comfortable. Old-world prettiness for women with a calmer lifestyle, *opposite*, a flowered chiffon nightdress with lace edging, peach ribbons, very much at home in this countrified setting.

BV 1974 Arthur Elgort. *Vignettes/Antiquarius*

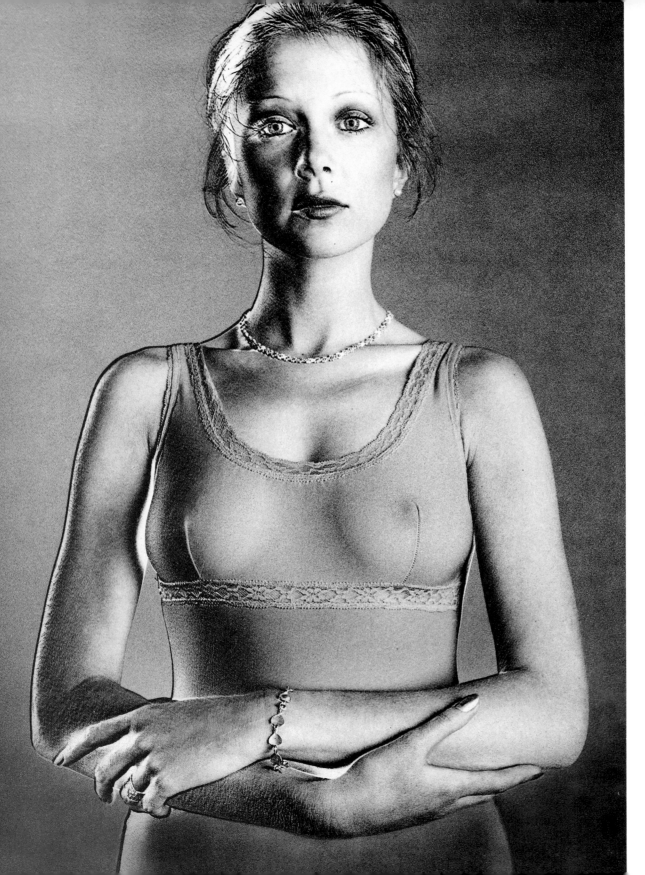

BV 1971 David Bailey. *Christian Dior*

Very fine, very stretchy, the softest bra of the decade for the bra-less look, *left,* was called a cami-vest. The varied lingerie mode, *opposite,* of 1974. Natural-look bras and lightly elasticated knickers, *below,* contrast with the firmer control of the long-line and swimsuit-shaped foundations *above.* The two full-length drawings show the frilly knickerbockers which were a shortlived fashion of the time, knee-length petticoat, a low-cut bra with the fashionable wide-set straps, and a laced, long-line bra, giving a softly natural silhouette like that of the bra *on this page.*

BV 1971 Caroline Smith. *Left to right: above, Silhouette; below, Lovable* (bra), *Kayser* (girdle); *Madeleine; above, Berlei; below, Triumph; Silhouette*

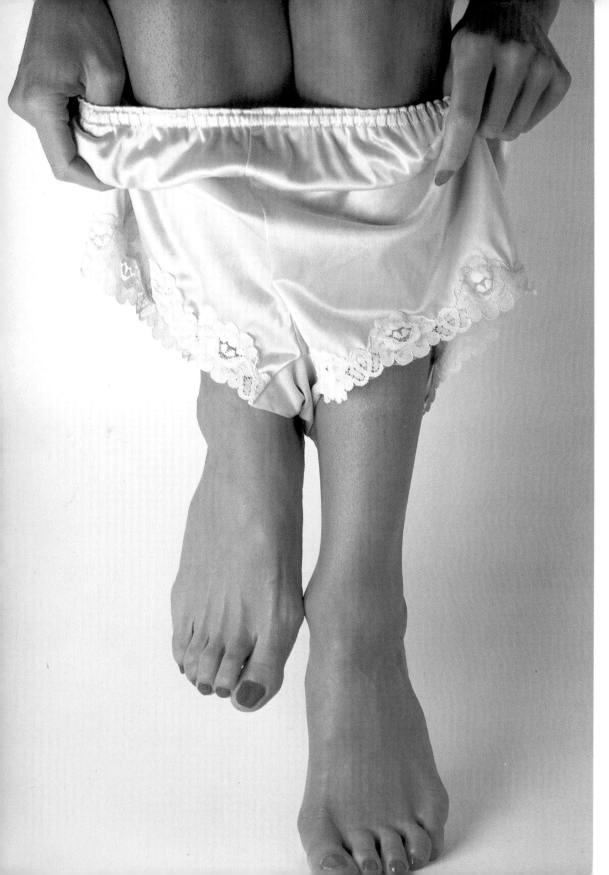

Australian *Vogue* 1976
Warren Scott

Gilding the lily, *on this page*,
with the addition of these
lacy, silky French knickers.
Reversal of the process,
opposite, as all is revealed.
The front-fastening bra,
made entirely of lacy net on
an elasticated band for
minimum weight, is cut low
at the cleavage.

BV 1977 Irving Penn

BV 1973 Norman Parkinson.
Bill Gibb

Softly draping nightwear, dressed up for the boudoir. Cream Quiana jersey night-gown, *on this page,* with lace halter and edges, the bib embroidered with coffee 'leaves'. Frill on frill of chiffon make a soft, dressy nightgown in forget-me-not blue and palest cream, *opposite.*

BV 1973 Norma Parkinson.
Gina Fratini

Sensuous silks and ultrafine hose
for these feminized, vampish
sailors. French knickers, crepe
de chine bras are suspended on a
length of lanyard to dry.

FV 1979 Guy Bourdin.
Annabelle, Christian Dior,
Nuits d'Elodie,
Claude Montana (clothes)

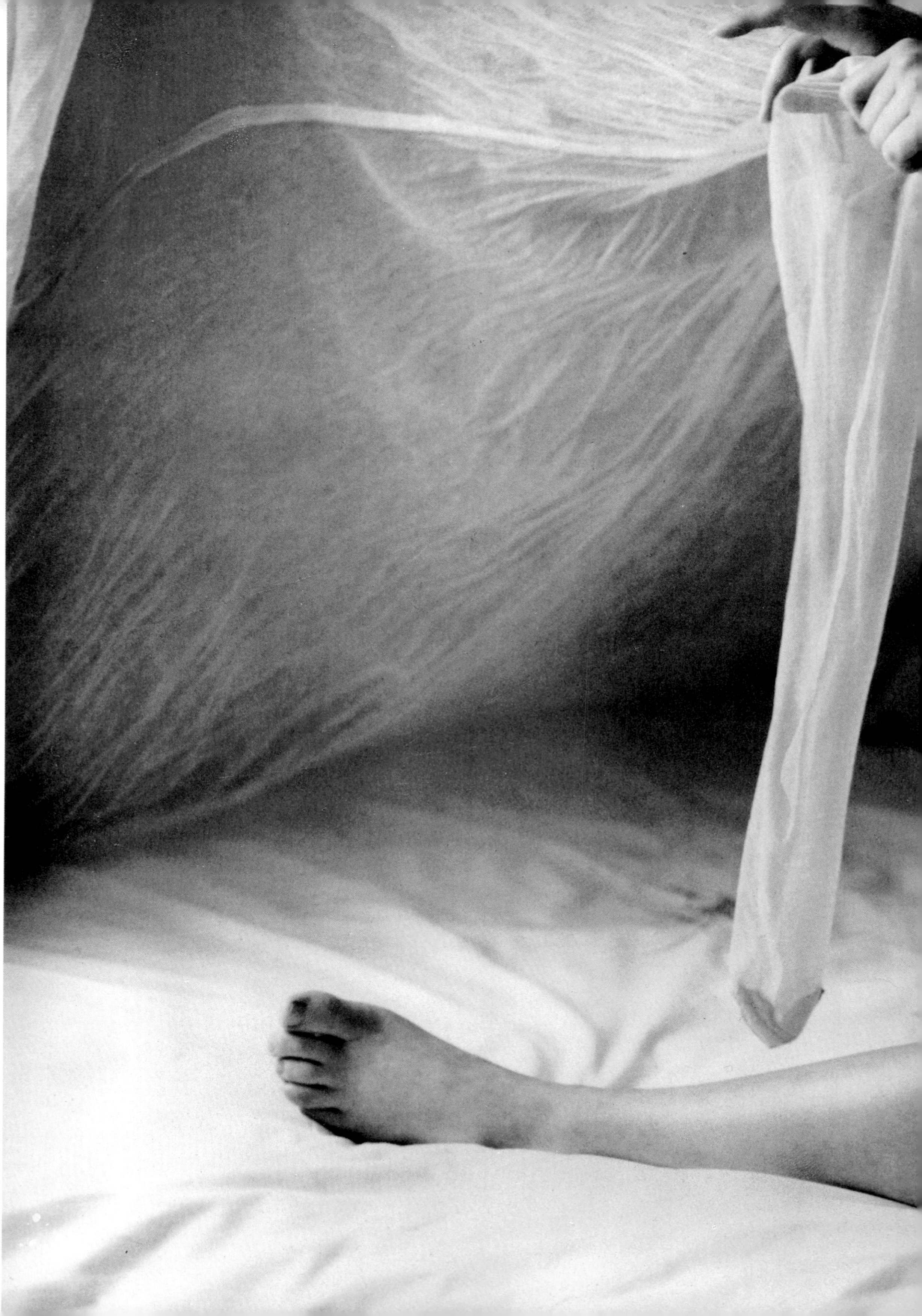

Seventies-style
camisole, wrapover
crepe de chine, *right,*
worn with French
knickers as underwear,
nightwear, boudoir
wear. The simple,
uncluttered line is
typical of the late
seventies and early
eighties, when fashion
became more tailored
and close-fitting, yet
lost nothing in
sensuality.

BV 1980 John Stember.
Janet Reger

BV 1977 Eric Boman. *Zandra Rhodes*

Silk lingerie in a devastating blend: attractive, erotic, practical. Slimmest silk-satin French knickers, *opposite*, were evening and everyday fashion as the eighties dawned; they flattered the body, were soft to wear. Palest pink satin and cream lace camiknickers, *above*, decorated the naked body, rather than dressing it.

Overleaf: the ultimate erotic undercover. GV 1979 Claus Wickrath

FV 1980 Mike Reinhardt